The Little Book on CoffeeScript

Alex MacCaw

O'REILLY®

Beijing · Cambridge · Farnham · Köln · Sebastopol · Tokyo

The Little Book on CoffeeScript
by Alex MacCaw

Published by O'Reilly Media, Inc., 1005 Gravenstein Highway North, Sebastopol, CA 95472.

O'Reilly books may be purchased for educational, business, or sales promotional use. Online editions are also available for most titles (*http://my.safaribooksonline.com*). For more information, contact our corporate/institutional sales department: (800) 998-9938 or *corporate@oreilly.com*.

Editor: Mary Treseler
Production Editor: Jasmine Perez
Proofreader: O'Reilly Production Services

Cover Designer: Karen Montgomery
Interior Designer: David Futato
Illustrator: Robert Romano

Revision History for the First Edition:
2012-01-17   First release
See *http://oreilly.com/catalog/errata.csp?isbn=9781449321055* for release details.

ISBN: 978-1-449-32105-5

[LSI]

1326293672

Table of Contents

Preface

What Is CoffeeScript?

CoffeeScript (*http://coffeescript.org*) is a little language that compiles down to Java-Script. The syntax is inspired by Ruby and Python, and implements many features from those two languages. This book is designed to help you learn CoffeeScript, understand best practices, and start building awesome client-side applications. The book is little, only six chapters, but that's rather apt as CoffeeScript is a little language too.

This book is completely open source, and was written by Alex MacCaw (*http://alex maccaw.co.uk*) (@maccman (*http://twitter.com/maccman*)) with great contributions from David Griffiths (*https://github.com/dxgriffiths*), Satoshi Murakami (*http://github .com/satyr*), Chris Smith (*http://www.coffeescriptlove.com*), Katsuya Noguchi (*http:// about.me/knoguchi*), and Jeremy Ashkenas (*https://github.com/jashkenas*).

If you have any errata or suggestions, please don't hesitate to open a ticket on the book's GitHub page (*https://github.com/arcturo/library*). Readers may also be interested in JavaScript Web Applications (*http://shop.oreilly.com/product/0636920018421.do*) (O'Reilly), a book I authored that explores rich JavaScript applications and moving state to the client side.

So let's dive right into it: why is CoffeeScript better than writing pure JavaScript? Well, for a start, there's less code to write; CoffeeScript is very succinct, and takes white space into account. In my experience, this reduces code by a third to a half of the original pure JavaScript. In addition, CoffeeScript has some neat features, such as array comprehensions, prototype aliases, and classes that further reduce the amount of typing you need to do.

More importantly though, JavaScript has a lot of skeletons in its closet (*http://bonsaiden .github.com/JavaScript-Garden/*) which can often trip up inexperienced developers. CoffeeScript neatly sidesteps these by only exposing a curated selection of JavaScript features, fixing many of the language's oddities.

CoffeeScript is *not* a superset of JavaScript, so although you can use external JavaScript libraries from inside CoffeeScript, you'll get syntax errors if you compile JavaScript as is, without converting it. The compiler converts CoffeeScript code into its counterpart JavaScript, there's no interpretation at runtime.

So let's get some common fallacies out of the way. You will need to know JavaScript in order to write CoffeeScript, as runtime errors require JavaScript knowledge. However, having said that, runtime errors are usually pretty obvious, and so far I haven't found mapping JavaScript back to CoffeeScript to be an issue. The second problem I've often heard associated with CoffeeScript is speed (i.e., the code produced by the CoffeeScript compiler would run slower than its equivalent written in pure JavaScript). In practice though, it turns out this isn't a problem either. CoffeeScript tends to run as fast or faster than handwritten JavaScript.

What are the disadvantages of using CoffeeScript? Well, it introduces another compile step between you and your JavaScript. CoffeeScript tries to mitigate the issue as best it can by producing clean and readable JavaScript, and with its server integrations which automate compilation. The other disadvantage, as with any new language, is the fact that the community is still small at this point, and you'll have a hard time finding fellow collaborators who already know the language. CoffeeScript is quickly gaining momentum though, and its IRC list is well staffed; any questions you have are usually answered promptly.

CoffeeScript is not limited to the browser, and can be used to great effect in server-side JavaScript implementations, such as Node.js (*http://nodejs.org/*). Additionally, Coffee-Script is getting much wider use and integration, such as being a default in Rails 3.1. Now is definitely the time to jump on the CoffeeScript train. The time you invest in learning about the language now will be repaid by major time savings later.

Initial Setup

One of the easiest ways to initially play around with the library is to use it right inside the browser. Navigate to *http://coffeescript.org* and click on the *Try CoffeeScript* tab. The site uses a browser version of the CoffeeScript compiler, converting any CoffeeScript typed inside the left panel to JavaScript in the right panel.

You can also convert JavaScript back to CoffeeScript using the js2coffee (*http://js2coffee .org/*) project, especially useful when migrating JavaScript projects to CoffeeScript.

In fact, you can use the browser-based CoffeeScript compiler yourself, by including this script (*http://jashkenas.github.com/coffee-script/extras/coffee-script.js*) in a page, marking up any CoffeeScript script tags with the correct type:

```
<script src="http://jashkenas.github.com/coffee-script/extras/coffee-script.js"
type="text/javascript" charset="utf-8"></script>
<script type="text/coffeescript">
  # Some CoffeeScript
</script>
```

Obviously, in production, you don't want to be interpreting CoffeeScript at runtime, as it'll slow things up for your clients. Instead, CoffeeScript offers a Node.js (*http://nodejs.org*) compiler to pre-process CoffeeScript files.

To install it, first make sure you have a working copy of the latest stable version of Node.js (*http://nodejs.org*) and npm (*http://npmjs.org/*) (the Node Package Manager). You can then install CoffeeScript with npm:

```
npm install -g coffee-script
```

The -g flag is important, as it tells npm to install the coffee-script package globally, rather than locally. Without it, you won't get the coffee executable.

If you execute the coffee executable without any command line options, it'll give you the CoffeeScript console, which you can use to quickly execute CoffeeScript statements. To pre-process files, pass the --compile option:

```
coffee --compile my-script.coffee
```

If --output is not specified, CoffeeScript will write to a JavaScript file with the same name, in this case my-script.js. This will overwrite any existing files, so be careful you're not overwriting any JavaScript files unintentionally. For a full list of the command line options available, pass --help.

You can also pass the --compile option a directory, and CoffeeScript will recursively compile every file with a .coffee extension:

```
coffee --output lib --compile src
```

If all this compilation seems like a bit of an inconvenience and bother, that's because it is. We'll be getting onto ways to solve this by automatically compiling CoffeeScript files, but first let's take a look at the language's syntax.

Conventions Used in This Book

The following typographical conventions are used in this book:

Italic
> Indicates new terms, URLs, email addresses, filenames, and file extensions.

`Constant width`
> Used for program listings, as well as within paragraphs to refer to program elements such as variable or function names, databases, data types, environment variables, statements, and keywords.

`Constant width bold`
> Shows commands or other text that should be typed literally by the user.

`Constant width italic`
> Shows text that should be replaced with user-supplied values or by values determined by context.

This icon signifies a tip, suggestion, or general note.

 This icon indicates a warning or caution.

Using Code Examples

This book is here to help you get your job done. In general, you may use the code in this book in your programs and documentation. You do not need to contact us for permission unless you're reproducing a significant portion of the code. For example, writing a program that uses several chunks of code from this book does not require permission. Selling or distributing a CD-ROM of examples from O'Reilly books does require permission. Answering a question by citing this book and quoting example code does not require permission. Incorporating a significant amount of example code from this book into your product's documentation does require permission.

We appreciate, but do not require, attribution. An attribution usually includes the title, author, publisher, and ISBN. For example: "*The Little Book on CoffeeScript* by Alex MacCaw (O'Reilly). Copyright 2012 Alex MacCaw, 978-1-449-32105-5."

If you feel your use of code examples falls outside fair use or the permission given above, feel free to contact us at *permissions@oreilly.com*.

Safari® Books Online

 Safari Books Online is an on-demand digital library that lets you easily search over 7,500 technology and creative reference books and videos to find the answers you need quickly.

With a subscription, you can read any page and watch any video from our library online. Read books on your cell phone and mobile devices. Access new titles before they are available for print, and get exclusive access to manuscripts in development and post feedback for the authors. Copy and paste code samples, organize your favorites, download chapters, bookmark key sections, create notes, print out pages, and benefit from tons of other time-saving features.

O'Reilly Media has uploaded this book to the Safari Books Online service. To have full digital access to this book and others on similar topics from O'Reilly and other publishers, sign up for free at *http://my.safaribooksonline.com*.

How to Contact Us

Please address comments and questions concerning this book to the publisher:

O'Reilly Media, Inc.
1005 Gravenstein Highway North
Sebastopol, CA 95472
800-998-9938 (in the United States or Canada)
707-829-0515 (international or local)
707-829-0104 (fax)

We have a web page for this book, where we list errata, examples, and any additional information. You can access this page at:

http://shop.oreilly.com/product/0636920024309.do

To comment or ask technical questions about this book, send email to:

bookquestions@oreilly.com

For more information about our books, courses, conferences, and news, see our website at *http://www.oreilly.com*.

Find us on Facebook: *http://facebook.com/oreilly*

Follow us on Twitter: *http://twitter.com/oreillymedia*

Watch us on YouTube: *http://www.youtube.com/oreillymedia*

## CHAPTER 1

CoffeeScript Syntax

Firstly, before we get any further into this section, I want to reiterate that while CoffeeScript's syntax is often identical with JavaScript's, it's not a superset, and therefore some JavaScript keywords, such as `function` and `var`, aren't permitted, and will throw syntax errors. If you're writing a CoffeeScript file, it needs to be pure CoffeeScript; you can't intermingle the two languages.

Why isn't CoffeeScript a superset? Well, the very fact that white space is significant in CoffeeScript programs prevents it from being a superset. And, once that decision's been made, the team decided you might as well go the full hog and deprecate some JavaScript keywords and features in the name of simplicity and in an effort to reduce many commonly occurring bugs.

What I find mind-blowing, in a meta sort of way, is that the CoffeeScript interpreter itself is actually written in CoffeeScript. It looks like the chicken or egg paradox has finally been solved!

Right, so firstly let's tackle the basic stuff. There are no semicolons in CoffeeScript, it'll add them automatically for you upon compilation. Semicolons were the cause of much debate in the JavaScript community, and behind some weird interpreter behavior (*http://bonsaiden.github.com/JavaScript-Garden/#core.semicolon*). Anyway, CoffeeScript resolves this problem for you by simply removing semicolons from its syntax, adding them as needed behind the scenes.

Comments are in the same format as Ruby comments, starting with a hash character:

```
# A comment
```

Multiline comments are also supported, and are brought forward to the generated JavaScript. They're enclosed by three hash characters:

```
###
  A multiline comment, perhaps a LICENSE.
###
```

As you're going through this book's examples, it may be worth pasting the CoffeeScript into the online compiler (*http://jashkenas.github.com/coffee-script/*) showing you the generated JavaScript.

As I briefly alluded to, white space is significant in CoffeeScript. In practice, this means that you can replace curly brackets ({}) with a tab. This takes inspiration from Python's syntax, and has the excellent side effect of ensuring that your script is formatted in a sane manner; otherwise it won't even compile!

Variables and Scope

CoffeeScript fixes one of the major bugbears with JavaScript, global variables. In JavaScript, it's all too easy to accidentally declare a global variable by forgetting to include var before the variable assignment. CoffeeScript solves this by simply removing global variables. Behind the scenes, CoffeeScript wraps up scripts with an anonymous function, keeping the local context, and automatically prefixes all variable assignments with var. For example, take this simple variable assignment in CoffeeScript:

```
myVariable = "test"
```

As you can see, the variable assignment is kept completely local; it's impossible to accidentally create a global variable. CoffeeScript actually takes this a step further, and makes it difficult to shadow a higher-level variable. This goes a great deal to prevent some of the most common mistakes developers make in JavaScript.

However, sometimes it's useful to create global variables. You can either do this by directly setting them as properties on the global object (window in browsers), or with the following pattern:

```
exports = this
exports.MyVariable = "foo-bar"
```

In the root context, this is equal to the global object, and by creating a local exports variable you're making it really obvious to anyone reading your code exactly which global variables a script is creating. Additionally, it paves the way for CommonJS modules, which we're going to cover later in the book.

Functions

CoffeeScript removes the rather verbose function statement, and replaces it with a thin arrow: ->. Functions can be one-liners or indented on multiple lines. The last expression in the function is implicitly returned. In other words, you don't need to use the return statement unless you want to return earlier inside the function.

With that in mind, let's take a look at an example:

```
func = -> "bar"
```

You can see in the resultant compilation, the `->` is turned into a `function` statement, and the `"bar"` string is automatically returned.

As mentioned earlier, there's no reason why we can't use multiple lines, as long as we indent the function body properly:

```
func = ->
  # An extra line
  "bar"
```

Function Arguments

How about specifying arguments? Well, CoffeeScript lets you do that by specifying arguments in parentheses before the arrow:

```
times = (a, b) -> a * b
```

CoffeeScript supports default arguments too. For example:

```
times = (a = 1, b = 2) -> a * b
```

You can also use splats to accept multiple arguments (denoted by ...):

```
sum = (nums...) ->
  result = 0
  nums.forEach (n) -> result += n
  result
```

In the example above, `nums` is an array of all the arguments passed to the function. It's not an `arguments` object, but rather a real array, so you don't need to concern yourself with `Array.prototype.splice` or `jQuery.makeArray()` if you want to manipulate it.

```
trigger = (events...) ->
  events.splice(1, 0, this)
  this.constructor.trigger.apply(events)
```

Function Invocation

Functions can be invoked exactly as in JavaScript, with parens (), `apply()`, or `call()`. However, like Ruby, CoffeeScript will automatically call functions if they are invoked with at least one argument:

```
a = "Howdy!"

alert a
# Equivalent to:
alert(a)

alert inspect a
# Equivalent to:
alert(inspect(a))
```

Although parenthesis is optional, I'd recommend using it if it's not immediately obvious what's being invoked, and with which arguments. In the last example, with inspect, I'd definitely recommend wrapping at least the inspect invocation in parens:

```
alert inspect(a)
```

If you don't pass any arguments with an invocation, CoffeeScript has no way of working out if you intend to invoke the function, or just treat it like a variable. In this respect, CoffeeScript's behavior differs from Ruby's, which always invokes references to functions, and is more similar to Python's. This has been the source of a few errors in my CoffeeScript programs, so it's worth keeping an eye out for cases where you intend to call a function without any arguments, and include parenthesis.

Function Context

Context changes are rife within JavaScript, especially with event callbacks, so CoffeeScript provides a few helpers to manage this. One such helper is a variation on ->, the fat arrow function: =>

Using the fat arrow instead of the thin arrow ensures that the function context will be bound to the local one. For example:

```
this.clickHandler = -> alert "clicked"
element.addEventListener "click", (e) => this.clickHandler(e)
```

The reason you might want to do this is that callbacks from addEventListener() are executed in the context of the element, i.e. this equals the element. If you want to keep this equal to the local context, without doing a self = this dance, fat arrows are the way to go.

This binding idea is a similar concept to jQuery's proxy() (*http://api.jquery.com/jQuery .proxy/*) or ES5's (*https://developer.mozilla.org/en/JavaScript/Reference/Global_Ob jects/Function/bind*) bind() functions.

Object Literals and Array Definition

Object literals can be specified exactly as in JavaScript, with a pair of braces and key/value statements. However, like with function invocation, CoffeeScript makes the braces optional. In fact, you can also use indentation and new lines instead of comma separation:

```
object1 = {one: 1, two: 2}

# Without braces
object2 = one: 1, two: 2

# Using new lines instead of commas
object3 =
  one: 1
  two: 2
```

```
User.create(name: "John Smith")
```

Likewise, arrays can use white space instead of comma separators, although the square brackets ([]) are still required:

```
array1 = [1, 2, 3]

array2 = [
  1
  2
  3
]

array3 = [1,2,3,]
```

As you can see in this example, CoffeeScript has also stripped the trailing comma in array3, another common source of cross-browser errors.

Flow Control

The convention of optional parentheses continues with CoffeeScript's `if` and `else` keywords:

```
if true == true
  "We're ok"

if true != true then "Panic"

# Equivalent to:
#   (1 > 0) ? "Ok" : "Y2K!"
if 1 > 0 then "Ok" else "Y2K!"
```

As you can see above, if the `if` statement is on one line, you'll need to use the `then` keyword so CoffeeScript knows when the block begins. Conditional operators (?:) are not supported; instead you should use a single line `if`/`else` statement.

CoffeeScript also includes a Ruby idiom of allowing suffixed `if` statements:

```
alert "It's cold!" if heat < 5
```

Instead of using the exclamation mark (!) for negation, you can also use the `not` keyword—which can sometimes make your code more readable, as exclamation marks can be easy to miss:

```
if not true then "Panic"
```

In the example above, we could also use the CoffeeScript's `unless` statement, the opposite of `if`:

```
unless true
  "Panic"
```

In a similar fashion to `not`, CoffeeScript also introduces the `is` statement, which translates to ===:

```
if true is 1
  "Type coercion fail!"
```

As an alternative to is not, you can use isnt:

```
if true isnt true
  alert "Opposite day!"
```

You may have noticed in these examples that CoffeeScript is converting == operators into === and != into !==. This is one of my favorite features of the language, and yet one of the most simple. What's the reasoning behind this? Well, frankly, JavaScript's type coercion is a bit odd, and its equality operator coerces types in order to compare them, leading to some confusing behaviors and the source of many bugs. There's a longer discussion on this topic in Chapter 6.

String Interpolation

CoffeeScript brings Ruby style string interpolation to JavaScript. Double quotes strings can contain #{} tags, which contain expressions to be interpolated into the string:

```
favorite_color = "Blue. No, yel..."
question = "Bridgekeeper: What... is your favorite color?
            Galahad: #{favorite_color}
            Bridgekeeper: Wrong!
            "
```

As you can see in this example, multiline strings are also allowed, without having to prefix each line with a +.

Loops and Comprehensions

Array iteration in JavaScript has a rather archaic syntax, reminiscent of an older language like C rather than a modern object-orientated one. The introduction of ES5 improved that situation somewhat, with the forEach() function, but that still requires a function call every iteration and is therefore much slower. Again, CoffeeScript comes to the rescue, with a beautiful syntax:

```
for name in ["Roger", "Roderick", "Brian"]
  alert "Release #{name}"
```

If you need the current iteration index, just pass an extra argument:

```
for name, i in ["Roger the pickpocket", "Roderick the robber"]
  alert "#{i} - Release #{name}"
```

You can also iterate on one line, using the postfix form:

```
release prisoner for prisoner in ["Roger", "Roderick", "Brian"]
```

As with Python comprehensions, you can filter them:

```
prisoners = ["Roger", "Roderick", "Brian"]
release prisoner for prisoner in prisoners when prisoner[0] is "R"
```

You can also use comprehensions for iterating over properties in objects. Instead of the in keyword, use of:

```
names = sam: seaborn, donna: moss
alert("#{first} #{last}") for first, last of names
```

The only low-level loop that CoffeeScript exposes is the while loop. This has similar behavior to the while loop in pure JavaScript, but has the added advantage that it returns an array of results (i.e. like the Array.prototype.map() function):

```
num = 6
minstrel = while num -= 1
  num + " Brave Sir Robin ran away"
```

Arrays

CoffeeScript takes inspiration from Ruby when it comes to array slicing by using ranges. Ranges are created by two numerical values, the first and last positions in the range, separated by .. or .... If a range isn't prefixed by anything, CoffeeScript expands it out into an array:

```
range = [1..5]
```

If, however, the range is specified immediately after a variable, CoffeeScript converts it into a slice() method call:

```
firstTwo = ["one", "two", "three"][0..1]
```

In the example above, the range returns a new array, containing only the first two elements of the original array. You can also use the same syntax for replacing an array segment with another array:

```
numbers = [0..9]
numbers[3..5] = [-3, -4, -5]
```

What's neat, is that JavaScript allows you to call slice() on strings too, so you can use ranges with string to return a new subset of characters:

```
my = "my string"[0..1]
```

Checking to see if a value exists inside an array is always a bore in JavaScript, particularly because indexOf() doesn't yet have full cross-browser support (Internet Explorer, I'm talking about you). CoffeeScript solves this with the in operator, for example:

```
words = ["rattled", "roudy", "rebbles", "ranks"]
alert "Stop wagging me" if "ranks" in words
```

Aliases and the Existential Operator

CoffeeScript includes some useful aliases to save some typing. One such alias is @, which can be used in place of this:

```
@saviour = true
```

Another is ::, which is an alias for prototype:

```
User::first = -> @records[0]
```

Using if for null checks in JavaScript is common, but has a few pitfalls in that empty strings and zero are both coerced into false, which can catch you out. CoffeeScript existential operator ? returns true unless a variable is null or undefined, similar to Ruby's nil?:

```
praise if brian?
```

You can also use it in place of the || operator:

```
velocity = southern ? 40
```

If you're using a null check before accessing a property, you can skip that by placing the existential operator right before it. This is similar to Active Support's try (*http:// guides.rubyonrails.org/active_support_core_extensions.html#try*) method:

```
blackKnight.getLegs()?.kick()
```

Similarly, you can check that a property is actually a function, and callable, by placing the existential operator right before the parens. If the property doesn't exist, or isn't a function, it simply won't get called:

```
blackKnight.getLegs().kick?()
```

## CHAPTER 2

CoffeeScript Classes

For some purists, classes in JavaScript seem to have the kind of effect that cloves of garlic have to Dracula; although, let's be honest, if you're that way inclined, you're unlikely to be reading a book on CoffeeScript. However, it turns out that classes are just as useful in JavaScript as they are in other languages and CoffeeScript provides a great abstraction.

Behind the scenes, CoffeeScript is using JavaScript's native prototype to create classes; adding a bit of syntactic sugar for static property inheritance and context persistence. As a developer, all that's exposed to you is the `class` keyword:

```
class Animal
```

In the example above, `Animal` is the name of the class, and also the name of the resultant variable that you can use to create instances. Behind the scenes, CoffeeScript is using constructor functions, which means you can instantiate classes using the new operator:

```
animal = new Animal
```

Defining constructors (functions that get invoked upon instantiation) is simple—just use a function named `constructor`. This is akin to using Ruby's `initialize` or Python's `__init__`:

```
class Animal
  constructor: (name) ->
    @name = name
```

In fact, CoffeeScript provides a shorthand for the common pattern of setting instance properties. By prefixing arguments with @, CoffeeScript will automatically set the arguments as instance properties in the constructor. Indeed, this shorthand will also work for normal functions outside classes. The example below is equivalent to the last example, where we set the instance properties manually:

```
class Animal
  constructor: (@name) ->
```

As you'd expect, any arguments passed on instantiation are proxied to the constructor function:

```
animal = new Animal("Parrot")
alert "Animal is a #{animal.name}"
```

Instance Properties

Adding additional instance properties to a class is very straightforward; it's exactly the same syntax as adding properties on an object. Just make sure properties are indented correctly inside the class body:

```
class Animal
  price: 5

  sell: (customer) ->

animal = new Animal
animal.sell(new Customer)
```

Context changes are rife within JavaScript, and in Chapter 1 we talked about how CoffeeScript can lock the value of this to a particular context using a fat arrow function: =>. This ensures that whatever context a function is called under, it'll always execute inside the context it was created in. CoffeeScript has extended support for fat arrows to classes, so by using a fat arrow for an instance method you'll ensure that it's invoked in the correct context, and that this is always equal to the current instance:

```
class Animal
  price: 5

  sell: =>
    alert "Give me #{@price} shillings!"

animal = new Animal
$("#sell").click(animal.sell)
```

As demonstrated in the example above, this is especially useful in event callbacks. Normally, the sell() function would be invoked in the context of the #sell element. However, by using fat arrows for sell(), we're ensuring the correct context is being maintained, and that this.price equals 5.

Static Properties

How about defining class (i.e., static) properties? Well, it turns out that inside a class definition, this refers to the class object. In other words, you can set class properties by setting them directly on this.

```
class Animal
  this.find = (name) ->

Animal.find("Parrot")
```

In fact, as you may remember, CoffeeScript aliases this to @, which lets you write static properties even more succinctly:

```
class Animal
  @find: (name) ->

Animal.find("Parrot")
```

Inheritance and Super

It wouldn't be a proper class implementation without some form of inheritance, and CoffeeScript doesn't disappoint. You can inherit from another class by using the extends keyword. In the example below, Parrot extends from Animal, inheriting all of its instance properties, such as alive():

```
class Animal
  constructor: (@name) ->

  alive: ->
    false

class Parrot extends Animal
  constructor: ->
    super("Parrot")

  dead: ->
    not @alive()
```

You'll notice that in the example above, we're using the super() keyword. Behind the scenes, this is translated into a function call on the class's parent prototype, invoked in the current context. In this case, it'll be Parrot.__super__.constructor.call(this, "Parrot");. In practice, this will have exactly the same effect as invoking super in Ruby or Python, invoking the overridden inherited function.

Unless you override the constructor, by default CoffeeScript will invoke the parent's constructor when instances are created.

CoffeeScript uses prototypal inheritance to automatically inherit all of a class's instance properties. This ensures that classes are dynamic; even if you add properties to a parent class after a child has been created, the property will still be propagated to all of its inherited children:

```
class Animal
  constructor: (@name) ->

class Parrot extends Animal

Animal::rip = true

parrot = new Parrot("Macaw")
alert("This parrot is no more") if parrot.rip
```

It's worth pointing out though that static properties are copied to subclasses, rather than inherited using prototype as instance properties are. This is due to implementation details with JavaScript's prototypal architecture, and is a difficult problem to work around.

Mixins

Mixins (*http://en.wikipedia.org/wiki/Mixin*) are not something supported natively by CoffeeScript, for the good reason that they can be trivially implemented yourself. For example, here's two functions, extend() and include(), that'll add class and instance properties respectively to a class:

```
extend = (obj, mixin) ->
  obj[name] = method for name, method of mixin
  obj

include = (klass, mixin) ->
  extend klass.prototype, mixin

# Usage
include Parrot,
  isDeceased: true

(new Parrot).isDeceased
```

Mixins are a great pattern for sharing common logic between modules when inheritance is not suitable. The advantage of mixins is that you can include multiple ones, compared to inheritance where only one class can be inherited from.

Extending Classes

Mixins are pretty neat, but they're not very object orientated. Instead, let's integrate mixins into CoffeeScript's classes. We're going to define a class called Module that we can inherit from for mixin support. Module will have two static functions, @extend() and @include(), which we can use for extending the class with static and instance properties, respectively:

```
moduleKeywords = ['extended', 'included']

class Module
  @extend: (obj) ->
    for key, value of obj when key not in moduleKeywords
      @[key] = value

    obj.extended?.apply(@)
    this

  @include: (obj) ->
    for key, value of obj when key not in moduleKeywords
      # Assign properties to the prototype
```

```
    @::[key] = value

  obj.included?.apply(@)
  this
```

The little dance around the moduleKeywords variable is to ensure we have callback support when mixins extend a class. Let's take a look at our Module class in action:

```
classProperties =
  find: (id) ->
  create: (attrs) ->

instanceProperties =
  save: ->

class User extends Module
  @extend classProperties
  @include instanceProperties

# Usage:
user = User.find(1)

user = new User
user.save()
```

As you can see, we've added some static properties, find() and create(), to the User class, as well as an instance property, save(). Since we've got callbacks whenever modules are extended, we can shortcut the process of applying both static and instance properties:

```
ORM =
  find: (id) ->
  create: (attrs) ->
  extended: ->
    @include
      save: ->

class User extends Module
  @extend ORM
```

Super simple and elegant!

## CHAPTER 3

CoffeeScript Idioms

Every language has a set of idioms and practices, and CoffeeScript is no exception. This chapter will explore those conventions, and show you some JavaScript to CoffeeScript comparisons so you can get a practical sense of the language.

Each

In JavaScript, to iterate over every item in an array, we could either use the newly added forEach() (*https://developer.mozilla.org/en/JavaScript/Reference/Global_Objects/array/foreach*) function, or an old C style for loop. If you're planning to use some of JavaScript's latest features introduced in ECMAScript 5, I advise you to also include a shim (*https://github.com/kriskowal/es5-shim*) in the page to emulate support in older browsers:

```
for (var i=0; i < array.length; i++)
  myFunction(array[i]);

array.forEach(function(item, i){
  myFunction(item)
});
```

Although the forEach() syntax is much more succinct and readable, it suffers from the drawback that the callback function will be invoked every iteration of the array, and is therefore much slower than the equivalent for loop. Let's see how it looks in CoffeeScript:

```
myFunction(item) for item in array
```

It's a readable and concise syntax, I'm sure you'll agree, and what's great is that it compiles to a for loop behind the scenes. In other words, CoffeeScript's syntax offers the same expressiveness as forEach(), but without the speed and shimming caveats.

Map

As with forEach(), ES5 also includes a native map function that has a much more succinct syntax than the classic for loop, namely map() (*https://developer.mozilla.org/en/JavaScript/Reference/Global_Objects/Array/map*). Unfortunately, it suffers from much the same caveats as forEach() (i.e., its speed is greatly reduced due to the function calls):

```
var result = []
for (var i=0; i < array.length; i++)
  result.push(array[i].name)

var result = array.map(function(item, i){
  return item.name;
});
```

As we covered in Chapter 1, CoffeeScript's comprehensions can be used to get the same behavior as map(). Notice we're surrounding the comprehension with parens, which is *absolutely critical* in ensuring the comprehension returns what you'd expect (i.e., the mapped array):

```
result = (item.name for item in array)
```

Select

Again, ES5 has a utility function filter() (*https://developer.mozilla.org/en/JavaScript/Reference/Global_Objects/array/filter*) for reducing arrays:

```
var result = []
for (var i=0; i < array.length; i++)
  if (array[i].name == "test")
    result.push(array[i])

result = array.filter(function(item, i){
  return item.name == "test"
});
```

CoffeeScript's basic syntax uses the when keyword to filter items with a comparison. Behind the scenes, a for loop is generated. The whole execution is performed in an anonymous function to ward against scope leakage and variable conflict:

```
result = (item for item in array when item.name is "test")
```

Don't forget to include the parens, as otherwise result will be the last item in the array. CoffeeScript's comprehensions are so flexible that they allow you to do powerful selections as in the following example:

```
passed = []
failed = []
(if score > 60 then passed else failed).push score for score in [49, 58, 76, 82, 88, 90]
```

```
# Or
passed = (score for score in scores when score > 60)
```

If comprehensions get too long, you can split them onto multiple lines:

```
passed = []
failed = []
for score in [49, 58, 76, 82, 88, 90]
  (if score > 60 then passed else failed).push score
```

Includes

Checking to see if a value is inside an array is typically done with `indexOf()`, which rather mind-bogglingly still requires a shim, as Internet Explorer hasn't implemented it:

```
var included = (array.indexOf("test") != -1)
```

CoffeeScript has a neat alternative to this which Pythonists may recognize, namely `in`:

```
included = "test" in array
```

Behind the scenes, CoffeeScript is using `Array.prototype.indexOf()`, and shimming if necessary, to detect if the value is inside the array. Unfortunately, this means the same in syntax won't work for strings. We need to revert back to using `indexOf()` and testing if the result is negative:

```
included = "a long test string".indexOf("test") isnt -1
```

Or even better, hijack the bitwise operator so we don't have to do a -1 comparison.

```
string   = "a long test string"
included = !!~ string.indexOf "test"
```

Property Iteration

To iterate over a bunch of properties in JavaScript, you'd use the `in` operator. For example:

```
var object = {one: 1, two: 2}
for(var key in object) alert(key + " = " + object[key])
```

However, as you've seen in the previous section, CoffeeScript has already reserved `in` for use with arrays. Instead, the operator has been renamed `of`, and can be used like thus:

```
object = {one: 1, two: 2}
alert("#{key} = #{value}") for key, value of object
```

As you can see, you can specify variables for both the property name, and its value, which is rather convenient.

Min/Max

This technique is not specific to CoffeeScript, but I thought it useful to demonstrate anyway. `Math.max` and `Math.min` take multiple arguments, so you can easily use `...` to pass an array to them, retrieving the maximum and minimum values in the array:

```
Math.max [14, 35, -7, 46, 98]... # 98
Math.min [14, 35, -7, 46, 98]... # -7
```

It's worth noting that this trick will fail with really large arrays, as browsers have a limitation on the amount of arguments you can pass to functions.

Multiple Arguments

In the `Math.max` example above, we're using `...` to de-structure the array and passing it as multiple arguments to `max`. Behind the scenes, CoffeeScript is converting the function call to use `apply()`, ensuring the array is passed as multiple arguments to `max`. We can use this feature in other ways too, such as proxying function calls:

```
Log =
  log: ->
    console?.log(arguments...)
```

Or you can alter the arguments before they're passed onwards:

```
Log =
  logPrefix: "(App)"

  log: (args...) ->
    args.unshift(@logPrefix) if @logPrefix
    console?.log(args...)
```

Bear in mind though that CoffeeScript will automatically set the function invocation context to the object the function is being invoked on. In the example above, that would be `console`. If you want to set the context specifically, then you'll need to call `apply()` manually.

And/Or

CoffeeScript style indicates that `or` is preferred over `||`, and `and` is preferred over `&&`. I can see why, as the former is somewhat more readable. Nevertheless, the two styles have identical results.

This preference for natural-language style code also applies to using `is` instead of `==` and `isnt` rather than `!=`:

```
string = "migrating coconuts"
string == string # true
string is string # true
```

One extremely nice addition to CoffeeScript is the "or equals", which is a pattern Rubyists may recognize as ||=:

```
hash or= {}
```

If hash evaluates to false, then it's set to an empty object. It's important to note here that this expression also recognizes 0, "", and null as false. If that isn't your intention, you'll need to use CoffeeScript's existential operator, which only gets activated if hash is undefined or null:

```
hash ?= {}
```

Destructuring Assignments

Destructuring assignments can be used with any depth of array and object nesting to help pull out deeply nested properties:

```
someObject = { a: 'value for a', b: 'value for b' }
{ a, b } = someObject
console.log "a is '#{a}', b is '#{b}'"
```

This is especially useful in Node applications when requiring modules:

```
{join, resolve} = require('path')

join('/Users', 'Alex')
```

External Libraries

Using external libraries is exactly the same as calling functions on CoffeeScript libraries because, at the end of the day, everything is compiled down to JavaScript. Using CoffeeScript with jQuery (*http://jquery.com*) is especially elegant, due to the amount of callbacks in jQuery's API:

```
# Use local alias
$ = jQuery

$ ->
  # DOMContentLoaded
  $(".el").click ->
    alert("Clicked!")
```

Since all of CoffeeScript's output is wrapped in an anonymous function, we can set a local $ alias for jQuery. This will make sure that even if jQuery's no conflict mode is enabled and the $ re-defined, our script will still function as intended.

Private Variables

The do keyword in CoffeeScript lets us execute functions immediately, a great way of encapsulating scope and protecting variables. In the example below, we're defining a variable classToType in the context of an anonymous function which is immediately called by do. That anonymous function returns a second anonymous function, which will be the ultimate value of type. Since classToType is defined in a context in which no reference is kept, it can't be accessed outside that scope:

```
# Execute function immediately
type = do ->

  types = [
    "Boolean"
    "Number"
    "String"
    "Function"
    "Array"
    "Date"
    "RegExp"
    "Undefined"
    "Null"
  ]

  classToType = {}
  for name in types
    classToType["[object " + name + "]"] = name.toLowerCase()

  # Return a function
  (obj) ->
    strType = Object::toString.call(obj)
    classToType[strType] or "object"
```

In other words, classToType is completely private, and can never again be referenced outside the executing anonymous function. This pattern is a great way of encapsulating scope and hiding variables.

## CHAPTER 4

Compiling CoffeeScript

An issue with CoffeeScript is that it puts another layer between you and JavaScript, and having to manually compile CoffeeScript files whenever they change quickly gets old. Fortunately, CoffeeScript has some alternative forms of compilation that can make the development cycle somewhat smoother.

As we covered in "Initial Setup" on page vi, we can compile CoffeeScript files using the coffee executable:

```
coffee --compile --output lib src
```

However, calling that whenever a source file changes is a bit of a bore, so let's look into automating it.

Cake

Cake (*http://jashkenas.github.com/coffee-script/#cake*) is a super simple build system along the lines of Make (*http://www.gnu.org/software/make/*) and Rake (*http://rake.ru byforge.org/*). The library is bundled with the coffee-script npm package, and available via an executable called cake.

You can define tasks using CoffeeScript in a file called Cakefile. Cake will pick these up, and can be invoked by running cake [task] [options] from within the directory. To print a list of all the tasks and options, just type cake.

Tasks are defined using the task() function, passing a name, optional description, and callback function. For example, create a file called Cakefile, and two directories, lib and src. Add the following to the Cakefile:

```
fs = require 'fs'

{print} = require 'util'
{spawn} = require 'child_process'

build = (callback) ->
  coffee = spawn 'coffee', ['-c', '-o', 'lib', 'src']
```

```
coffee.stderr.on 'data', (data) ->
  process.stderr.write data.toString()
coffee.stdout.on 'data', (data) ->
  print data.toString()
coffee.on 'exit', (code) ->
  callback?() if code is 0

task 'build', 'Build lib/ from src/', ->
  build()
```

In the example above, we're defining a task called `build` that can be invoked by running `cake build`. This runs the same command as the previous example, compiling all the CoffeeScript files in `src` to JavaScript in `lib`. You can now reference JavaScript files in the `lib` directory as per usual from your HTML:

```
<script src="lib/app.js" type="text/javascript" charset="utf-8"></script>
```

We're still having to manually run `cake build` whenever our CoffeeScript code changes, which is far from ideal. Luckily, the `coffee` command takes another option, `--watch`, which instructs it to watch a directory for changes and re-compiling as necessary. Let's define another task using that:

```
task 'watch', 'Watch src/ for changes', ->
  coffee = spawn 'coffee', ['-w', '-c', '-o', 'lib', 'src']
  coffee.stderr.on 'data', (data) ->
    process.stderr.write data.toString()
  coffee.stdout.on 'data', (data) ->
    print data.toString()
```

If one task relies on another, you can run other tasks using `invoke(name)`. Let's add a utility task to our `Cakefile` which is going to both open `index.html` and start watching the source for changes:

```
task 'open', 'Open index.html', ->
  # First open, then watch
  spawn 'open', 'index.html'
  invoke 'watch'
```

You can also define options for your task using the `option()` function, which takes a short name, long name, and description:

```
option '-o', '--output [DIR]', 'output dir'

task 'build', 'Build lib/ from src/', ->
  # Now we have access to a `options` object
  coffee = spawn 'coffee', ['-c', '-o', options.output or 'lib', 'src']
  coffee.stderr.on 'data', (data) ->
    process.stderr.write data.toString()
  coffee.stdout.on 'data', (data) ->
    print data.toString()
```

As you can see, the task context now has access to an `options` object containing any data specified by the user. If we run `cake` without any other arguments, all the tasks and options will be listed.

Cake's a great way of automating common tasks such as compiling CoffeeScript without going to the hassle of using bash or Makefiles. It's also worth taking a look at Cake's source (*http://jashkenas.github.com/coffee-script/documentation/docs/cake .html*), a great example of CoffeeScript's expressiveness and beautifully documented alongside the code comments.

Creating Applications

Using Cake for CoffeeScript compilation is fine for static sites, but for dynamic sites, we might as well integrate CoffeeScript compilation into the request/response cycle. Various integration solutions already exist for the popular backend languages and frameworks, such as Rails (*http://rubyonrails.org/*) and Django (*https://www.djangopro ject.com/*).

The rest of this chapter explores how to actually structure and deploy CoffeeScript client-side applications. If you're just using CoffeeScript on the server side, or your framework, such as Rails, already manages this, feel free to skip to Chapter 5.

For some reason, when developers build client-side JavaScript applications, tried and tested patterns and conventions often fly out the window, and the end result is a spaghetti mess of unmaintainable coupled JavaScript. I can't stress enough how important application architecture is; if you're writing any JavaScript/CoffeeScript beyond simple form validation, you should implement a form of application structure, such as MVC (*http://en.wikipedia.org/wiki/Model%E2%80%93view%E2%80%93con troller*).

The secret to building maintainable large applications is not to build large applications. In other words, build a series of modular de-coupled components. Keep application logic as generic as possible, abstracting it out as appropriate. Lastly, separate out your logic into views, models, and controllers (MVC). Implementing MVC is beyond the scope of this chapter; for that, I recommend you check out my book on JavaScript Web Applications and use a framework like Backbone (*http://documentcloud.github.com/ backbone/*) or Spine (*https://github.com/maccman/spine*). Rather than that, here we're going to cover structuring applications using CommonJS modules.

Structure and CommonJS

So what exactly are CommonJS modules? Well, If you've used NodeJS (*http://nodejs .org/*) before, you've used CommonJS modules, probably without realizing it. CommonJS modules were initially developed for writing server-side JavaScript libraries, in an attempt to deal with loading, namespacing, and scoping issues. They were a common format that would be compatible across all JavaScript implementations. The aim was that a library written for Rhino (*http://www.mozilla.org/rhino/*) would work for Node. Eventually these ideas transitioned back to browsers, and now we have great libraries like RequireJS (*http://requirejs.org*) and Yabble (*https://github.com/jbrantly/yabble*) to help us use modules on the client side.

Practically speaking, modules ensure that your code is run in a local namespace (code encapsulation), that you can load other modules with the require() function, and that you can expose module properties via module.exports. Let's dive into that in a bit more depth now.

Requiring files

You can load in other modules and libraries using require(). Simply pass a module name and, if it's in the load path, it'll return an object representing that module. For example:

```
User = require("models/user")
```

Synchronous require support is a contentious issue, but has mostly been resolved with the mainstream loader libraries and latest CommonJS proposals (*http://wiki.commonjs .org/wiki/Modules/AsynchronousDefinition*). It may be something you'll have to look into if you decided to take a separate route than the one I'm advocating with Stitch below.

Exporting properties

By default, modules don't expose any properties, so their contents are completely invisible to require() calls. If you want a particular property to be accessible from your module, you'll need to set it on module.exports:

```
# random_module.js
module.exports.myFineProperty = ->
  # Some shizzle
```

Now whenever this module is required, myFineProperty will be exposed:

```
myFineProperty = require("random_module").myFineProperty
```

Stitch It Up

Formatting your code as CommonJS modules is all fine and dandy, but how do you actually get this working on the client in practice? Well, my method of choice is the rather unheard of Stitch (*https://github.com/sstephenson/stitch*) library. Stitch is by Sam Stephenson, the mind behind Prototype.js (*http://www.prototypejs.org*) among other things, and solves the module problem so elegantly it makes me want to dance for joy! Rather than try to dynamically resolve dependencies, Stitch simply bundles up all your JavaScript files into one, wrapping them in some CommonJS magic. Oh, and did I mention it'll compile your CoffeeScript, JS templates, LESS CSS (*http://lesscss.org*), and Sass (*http://sass-lang.com*) files too?

First things first, you'll need to install Node.js (*http://nodejs.org/*) and npm (*http://npmjs .org/*) if you haven't already. We'll be using those throughout this chapter.

Now let's create our application structure. If you're using Spine (*https://github.com/maccman/spine*), you can automate this with Spine.App (*http://github.com/maccman/spine.app*); otherwise, it's something you'll need to do manually. I usually have an `app` folder for all the application specific code, and a `lib` folder for general libraries. Then anything else, including static assets, goes in the `public` directory:

```
app
app/controllers
app/views
app/models
app/lib
lib
public
public/index.html
```

Now to actually boot up the Stitch server. Let's create a file called `index.coffee` and fill it with the following script:

```
require("coffee-script")
stitch  = require("stitch")
express = require("express")
argv    = process.argv.slice(2)

package = stitch.createPackage(
  # Specify the paths you want Stitch to automatically bundle up
  paths: [ __dirname + "/app" ]

  # Specify your base libraries
  dependencies: [
    # __dirname + '/lib/jquery.js'
  ]
)
app = express.createServer()

app.configure ->
  app.set "views", __dirname + "/views"
  app.use app.router
  app.use express.static(__dirname + "/public")
  app.get "/application.js", package.createServer()

port = argv[0] or process.env.PORT or 9294
console.log "Starting server on port: #{port}"
app.listen port
```

You can see some dependencies listed: `coffee-script`, `stitch`, and `express`. We need to create a `package.json` file, listing these dependencies so npm can pick them up. Our `./package.json` file will look like this:

```
{
  "name": "app",
  "version": "0.0.1",
  "dependencies": {
    "coffee-script": "~1.1.2",
    "stitch": "~0.3.2",
    "express": "~2.5.0",
```

```
    "eco": "1.1.0-rc-1"
  }
}
```

And let's install those dependencies with npm:

```
npm install .
npm install -g coffee-script
```

Rightio, we're almost there. Now run:

```
coffee index.coffee
```

You'll hopefully have a Stitch server up and running. Let's go ahead and test it out by putting an `app.coffee` script in the app folder. This will be the file that'll bootstrap our application:

```
module.exports = App =
  init: ->
    # Bootstrap the app
```

Now let's create our main page `index.html` which, if we're building a single page app, will be the only page the user actually navigates to. This is a static asset, so it's located under the public directory:

```
<html>
<head>
  <meta charset=utf-8>
  <title>Application</title>
  <!-- Require the main Stitch file -->
  <script src="/application.js" type="text/javascript" charset="utf-8"></script>
  <script type="text/javascript" charset="utf-8">
    document.addEventListener("DOMContentLoaded", function(){
      var App = require("app");
      App.init();
    }, false);
  </script>
</head>
<body>
</body>
</html>
```

When the page loads, our *DOMContentLoaded* event callback is requiring the `app.coffee` script (which is automatically compiled), and invoking our `init()` function. That's all there is to it. We've got CommonJS modules up and running, as well as a HTTP server and CoffeeScript compiler. If, say, we wanted to include a module, it's just a case of calling `require()`. Let's create a new class, User, and reference it from `app.coffee`:

```
# app/models/user.coffee
module.exports = class User
  constructor: (@name) ->

# app/app.coffee
User = require("models/user")
```

JavaScript Templates

If you're moving logic to the client side, then you'll definitely need some sort of templating library. JavaScript templating is very similar to templates on the server, such as Ruby's ERB or Python's text interpolation, except of course it runs client side. There are a whole host of templating libraries out there, so I encourage you to do some research and check them out. By default, Stitch comes with support for Eco (*https://github.com/sstephenson/eco*) templates baked right in.

JavaScript templates are very similar to server-side ones. You have template tags inter-operated with HTML, and during rendering, those tags get evaluated and replaced. The great thing about Eco (*https://github.com/sstephenson/eco*) templates is they're actually written in CoffeeScript.

Here's an example:

```
<% if @projects.length: %>
  <% for project in @projects: %>
    <a href="<%= project.url %>"><%= project.name %></a>
    <p><%= project.description %></p>
  <% end %>
<% else: %>
  No projects
<% end %>
```

As you can see, the syntax is remarkably straightforward. Just use `<%` tags for evaluating expressions, and `<%=` tags for printing them. A partial list of template tags is as follows:

`<% expression %>`
Evaluate a CoffeeScript expression without printing its return value.

`<%= expression %>`
Evaluate a CoffeeScript expression, escape its return value, and print it.

`<%- expression %>`
Evaluate a CoffeeScript expression and print its return value without escaping it.

You can use any CoffeeScript expression inside the templating tags, but there's one thing to look out for. CoffeeScript is white space sensitive, but your Eco templates aren't. Therefore, Eco template tags that begin an indented CoffeeScript block must be suffixed with a colon. To indicate the end of an indented block, use the special tag `<% end %>`. For example:

```
<% if @project.isOnHold(): %>
  On Hold
<% end %>
```

You don't need to write the `if` and `end` tags on separate lines:

```
<% if @project.isOnHold(): %> On Hold <% end %>
```

And you can use the single-line postfix form of `if` as you'd expect:

```
<%= "On Hold" if @project.isOnHold() %>
```

Now that we've got a handle on the syntax, let's define an Eco template in views/users/show.eco:

```
<label>Name: <%= @name %></label>
```

Stitch will automatically compile our template and include it in application.js. Then, in our application's controllers, we can require the template, like it was a module, and execute it passing any data required:

```
require("views/users/show")(new User("Brian"))
```

Our app.coffee file should now look like this, rendering the template and appending it to the page when the document loads:

```
User = require("models/user")

App =
  init: ->
    template = require("views/users/show")
    view     = template(new User("Brian"))

    # Obviously this could be spruced up by jQuery
    element = document.createElement("div")
    element.innerHTML = view
    document.body.appendChild(element)

module.exports = App
```

Open up the application (*http://localhost:9294/*) and give it a whirl! Hopefully this tutorial has given you a good idea of how to structure client-side CoffeeScript applications. For your next steps, I recommend checking out a client-side framework like Backbone (*http://documentcloud.github.com/backbone/*) or Spine (*http://spinejs.com*), They'll provide a basic MVC structure for you, freeing you up for the interesting stuff.

Bonus: 30-Second Deployment with Heroku

Heroku (*http://heroku.com/*) is an incredibly awesome web host that manages all the servers and scaling for you, letting you get on with the exciting stuff (building awesome JavaScript applications). You'll need an account with Heroku for this tutorial to work, but the great news is that their basic plan is completely free. While traditionally a Ruby host, Heroku have recently released their Cedar stack, which includes Node support.

First, we need to make a Procfile, which will inform Heroku about our application:

```
echo "web: coffee index.coffee" > Procfile
```

Now, if you haven't already, you'll need to create a local git repository for your application:

```
git init
git add .
git commit -m "First commit"
```

And now to deploy the application, we'll use the `heroku` gem (which you'll need to install if you haven't already).

```
heroku create myAppName --stack cedar
git push heroku master
heroku open
```

That's it! Seriously, that's all there is to it. Hosting Node applications has never been easier.

Additional Libraries

Stitch (*https://github.com/sstephenson/stitch*) and Eco (*https://github.com/sstephenson/eco*) aren't the only libraries you can use for creating CoffeeScript and Node applications. There are a variety of alternatives.

For example, when it comes to templating, you can use Mustache (*http://mustache.github.com*), Jade (*http://jade-lang.com*), or write your HTML in pure CoffeeScript using CoffeeKup (*http://coffeekup.org*).

As for serving your application, Hem (*http://github.com/maccman/hem*) is a great choice, supporting both CommonJS and NPM modules and integrating seamlessly with the CoffeeScript MVC framework Spine (*http://spinejs.com*). node-browsify (*https://github.com/substack/node-browserify*) is another similar project. Or if you want to go lower level with express (*http://expressjs.com/*) integration, there's Trevor Burnham's connect-assets (*https://github.com/TrevorBurnham/connect-assets*)

You can find a full list of CoffeeScript web framework plug-ins on the project's wiki (*https://github.com/jashkenas/coffee-script/wiki/Web-framework-plugins*).

## CHAPTER 5

The Good Parts

JavaScript is a tricky beast, and knowing the parts that you should avoid is just as important as knowing about the parts you should use. As Sun Tzu says, "know your enemy," and that's exactly what we're going to do in the chapter, exploring the dark side of JavaScript and revealing some of the lurking monsters ready to pounce on the unsuspecting developer.

As I mentioned in the Preface, CoffeeScript's awesomeness lies not only in its syntax, but in its ability to fix some of JavaScript's warts. However, the language is not a silver bullet to all of JavaScript's bugbears, and there are still some issues you need to be aware of.

The Unfixed parts

While CoffeeScript goes some length to solving some of JavaScript's design flaws, it can only go so far. As I mentioned previously, CoffeeScript is strictly limited to static analysis by design, and doesn't do any runtime checking for performance reasons. CoffeeScript uses a straight source-to-source compiler, the idea being that every CoffeeScript statement results in an equivalent JavaScript statement. CoffeeScript doesn't provide an abstraction over any of JavaScript's keywords, such as typeof, and as such, some design flaws in JavaScript's design also apply to CoffeeScript.

We're going to first talk about some issues that CoffeeScript can't fix, and then touch on a few JavaScript design flaws that CoffeeScript does fix.

Using eval

While CoffeeScript removes some of JavaScript's foibles, other features are a necessary evil; you just need to be aware of their shortcomings. A case in point is the eval() function. While undoubtedly it has its uses, you should know about its drawbacks, and avoid it if possible. The eval() function will execute a string of JavaScript code in the local scope, and functions like setTimeout() and setInterval() can also both take a string as their first argument to be evaluated.

However, like with, eval() throws the compiler off track, and is a major performance hog. As the compiler has no idea what's inside until runtime, it can't perform any optimizations like inlining. Another concern is with security. If you give it dirty input, eval can easily open up your code for injection attacks. In almost every case, if you're using eval, there are better and safer alternatives (such as square brackets):

```
# Don't do this
model = eval(modelName)

# Use square brackets instead
model = window[modelName]
```

Using typeof

The typeof operator is probably the biggest design flaw of JavaScript, simply because it's basically completely broken. In fact, it really has only one use—checking to see if a value is undefined:

```
typeof undefinedVar is "undefined"
```

For all other types of type checking, typeof fails rather miserably, returning inconsistent results depending on the browser and how instances were instantiated. This isn't something that CoffeeScript can help you with either, since the language uses static analysis and has no runtime type checking. You're on your own here.

To illustrate the problem, here's a table taken from JavaScript Garden (*http://bonsaiden .github.com/JavaScript-Garden/*) which shows some of the major inconsistencies in the keyword's type checking:

```
Value                  Class       Type
------------------------------------------
"foo"                  String      string
new String("foo")      String      object
1.2                    Number      number
new Number(1.2)        Number      object
true                   Boolean     boolean
new Boolean(true)      Boolean     object
new Date()             Date        object
new Error()            Error       object
[1,2,3]                Array       object
new Array(1, 2, 3)     Array       object
new Function("")       Function    function
/abc/g                 RegExp      object
new RegExp("meow")     RegExp      object
{}                     Object      object
new Object()           Object      object
```

As you can see, depending on if you define a string with quotes or with the `String` class affects the result of `typeof`. Logically `typeof` should return `"string"` for both checks, but for the latter it returns `"object"`. Unfortunately, the inconsistencies only get worse from there.

So what can we use for type checking in JavaScript? Well, luckily `Object.prototype.toString()` comes to the rescue here. If we invoke that function in the context of a particular object, it'll return the correct type. All we need to do is massage the string it returns, so we end up with the sort of string `typeof` should be returning. Here's an example implementation ported from jQuery's `$.type`:

```coffeescript
type = do ->
  classToType = {}

  types = [
    "Boolean"
    "Number"
    "String"
    "Function"
    "Array"
    "Date"
    "RegExp"
    "Undefined"
    "Null"
  ]

  for name in types
    classToType["[object #{name}]"] = name.toLowerCase()

  (obj) ->
    strType = Object::toString.call(obj)
    classToType[strType] or "object"

# Returns the sort of types we'd expect:
type("")         # "string"
type(new String) # "string"
type([])         # "array"
type(/\d/)       # "regexp"
type(new Date)   # "date"
type(true)       # "boolean"
type(null)       # "null"
type({})         # "object"
```

If you're checking to see if a variable has been defined, you'll still need to use `typeof`; otherwise, you'll get a `ReferenceError`:

```coffeescript
if typeof aVar isnt "undefined"
  objectType = type(aVar)
```

Or more succinctly with the existential operator:

```coffeescript
objectType = type(aVar?)
```

As an alternative to type checking, you can often use duck typing and the CoffeeScript existential operator together, which eliminates the need to resolve an object's type. For example, let's say we're pushing a value onto an array. We could say that, as long as the "array like" object implements push(), we should treat it like an array:

```
anArray?.push? aValue
```

If anArray is an object other than an array, then the existential operator will ensure that push() is never called.

Using instanceof

JavaScript's instanceof keyword is nearly as broken as typeof. Ideally, instanceof would compare the constructor of two objects, returning a boolean if one was an instance of the other. However, in reality, instanceof only works when comparing custom-made objects. When it comes to comparing built-in types, it's as useless as typeof:

```
new String("foo") instanceof String # true
"foo" instanceof String            # false
```

Additionally, instanceof also doesn't work when comparing objects from different frames in the browser. In fact, instanceof only returns a correct result for custom made objects, such as CoffeeScript classes:

```
class Parent
class Child extends Parent

child = new Child
child instanceof Child  # true
child instanceof Parent # true
```

Make sure you only use it for your own objects or, even better, stay clear of it.

Using delete

The delete keyword can only safely be used for removing properties inside objects:

```
anObject = {one: 1, two: 2}
delete anObject.one
anObject.hasOwnProperty("one") # false
```

Any other use, such as deleting variables or function's won't work:

```
aVar = 1
delete aVar
typeof aVar # "integer"
```

It's rather peculiar behavior, but there you have it. If you want to remove a reference to a variable, just assign it to null instead:

```
aVar = 1
aVar = null
```

Using parseInt

JavaScript's `parseInt()` function can return unexpected results if you pass a string to it without informing it of the proper base. For example:

```
# Returns 8, not 10!
parseInt('010') is 8
```

Always pass a base to the function to make it work correctly:

```
# Use base 10 for the correct result
parseInt('010', 10) is 10
```

This isn't something CoffeeScript can do for you; you'll just have to remember to always specify a base when using `parseInt()`.

Strict Mode

Strict mode is a new feature of ECMAScript 5 that allows you to run a JavaScript program or function in a *strict* context. This strict context throws more exceptions and warnings than the normal context, giving developers some indication when they're straying from best practices, writing un-optimizable code or making common mistakes. In other words, strict mode reduces bugs, increases security, improves performance, and eliminates some difficult-to-use language features. What's not to like?

Strict mode is currently supported in the following browsers:

- Chrome >= 13.0
- Safari >= 5.0
- Opera >= 12.0
- Firefox >= 4.0
- Internet Explorer >= 10.0

Having said that, strict mode is completely backwards compatible with older browsers. Programs using it should run fine in either a strict or normal context.

Strict Mode Changes

Most of the changes strict mode introduces pertain to JavaScript's syntax:

- Errors on duplicate property and function argument names
- Errors on incorrect use of the `delete` operator
- Access to `arguments.caller` & `arguments.callee` throws an error (for performance reasons)
- Using the `with` operator will raise a syntax error
- Certain variables such as `undefined` are no longer writeable

- Introduces additional reserved keywords, such as `implements`, `interface`, `let`, `package`, `private`, `protected`, `public`, `static`, and `yield`

However, strict mode also changes some runtime behavior:

- Global variables are explicit (`var` always required); the global value of `this` is `undefined`
- `eval` can't introduce new variables into the local context
- Function statements have to be defined before they're used (previously, functions could be defined anywhere (*http://whereswalden.com/2011/01/24/new-es5-strict-mode-requirement-function-statements-not-at-top-level-of-a-program-or-function-are-prohibited/*))
- `arguments` is immutable

CoffeeScript already abides by a lot of strict mode's requirements, such as always using `var` when defining variables, but it's still very useful to enable strict mode in your CoffeeScript programs. Indeed, CoffeeScript is taking this a step further, and in future versions (*https://github.com/jashkenas/coffee-script/issues/1547*) will check a program's compliance to strict mode at compile time.

Strict Mode Usage

All you need to do to enable strict checking is start your script or function with the following string:

```
->
  "use strict"

  # ... your code ...
```

That's it, just the `"use strict"` string. Couldn't be simpler and it's completely backwards compatible. Let's take a look at strict mode in action. The following function will raise a syntax error in strict mode, but run fine in the usual mode:

```
do ->
  "use strict"
  console.log(arguments.callee)
```

Strict mode has removed access to `arguments.caller` and `arguments.callee`, as they're major performance hogs, and is now throwing syntax errors whenever they're used.

There's a particular gotcha you should look out for when using strict mode, namely creating global variables with `this`. The following example will throw a `TypeError` in strict mode, but run fine in a normal context, creating a global variable:

```
do ->
  "use strict"
  class @Spine
```

The reason behind this disparity is that in strict mode, `this` is `undefined`, whereas normally it refers to the `window` object. The solution to this is to explicitly set global variables on the `window` object:

```
do ->
  "use strict"
  class window.Spine
```

While I recommend enabling strict mode, it's worth noting that script mode doesn't enable any new features that aren't already possible in JavaScript, and will actually slow down your code a bit by having the VM do more checks at runtime. You may want to develop with strict mode, and deploy to production without it.

The Fixed Parts

Now that we've covered some of JavaScript's warts that CoffeeScript can't fix, let's talk about a few that CoffeeScript does fix. In my mind, the following features are some of the best reasons to use CoffeeScript; they fix some of the most common mistakes developers make when writing JavaScript. While this is more of an academic discussion, you should still find the rest of this chapter useful, especially when making the case to use CoffeeScript!

A JavaScript Subset

CoffeeScript's syntax only covers a subset of JavaScript's, the famous *Good Parts*, so already there's less to fix. Let's take the `with` statement for example. This statement has for a long time been "considered harmful," and should be avoided. `with` was intended to provide a shorthand for writing recurring property lookups on objects. For example, instead of writing:

```
dataObj.users.alex.email = "info@eribium.org";
```

You could write:

```
with(dataObj.users.alex) {
  email = "info@eribium.org";
}
```

Setting aside the fact that we shouldn't have such a deep object in the first place, the syntax is quite clean. Except for one thing. It's confusing to the JavaScript interpreter, which doesn't know exactly what you're going to do in the `with` context, and forces the specified object to be searched first for all name lookups.

This really hurts performance and means the interpreter has to turn off all sorts of JIT optimizations. Additionally, `with` statements can't be minified using tools like uglify-js (*https://github.com/mishoo/UglifyJS*). They're also deprecated and removed from future JavaScript versions. All things considered, it's much better just to avoid using them, and CoffeeScript takes this a step further by eliminating them from its syntax. In other words, using `with` in CoffeeScript will throw a syntax error.

Global Variables

By default, your JavaScript programs run in a global scope, and by default, any variables created are in that global scope. If you want to create a variable in the local scope, JavaScript requires explicitly indicating that fact using the `var` keyword.

```
usersCount = 1;         // Global
var groupsCount = 2;    // Global

(function(){
  pagesCount = 3;       // Global
  var postsCount = 4;   // Local
})()
```

This is a bit of an odd decision since the vast majority of the time you'll be creating local variables not global ones, so why not make that the default? As it stands, developers have to remember to put `var` statements before any variables they're initializing, or face weird bugs when variables accidentally conflict and overwrite each other.

Luckily, CoffeeScript comes to your rescue here by eliminating implicit global variable assignment entirely. In other words, the `var` keyword is reserved in CoffeeScript, and will trigger a syntax error if used. Local variables are created implicitly by default, and it's very difficult to create global variables without explicitly assigning them as properties on `window`.

Let's have a look at an example of CoffeeScript's variable assignment:

```
outerScope = true
do ->
  innerScope = true
```

Compiles down to:

```
var outerScope;
outerScope = true;
(function() {
  var innerScope;
  return innerScope = true;
})();
```

Notice how CoffeeScript initializes variables (using `var`) automatically in the context they are first used. While CoffeeScript makes it difficult to shadow outer variables, you can still refer to and access them. You need to watch out for this; be careful that you're not reusing the name of an external variable accidentally if you're writing a deeply nested function or class. For example, here we're accidentally overwriting the package variable in a Class function:

```
package = require('./package')

class Hem
```

```
build: ->
  # Overwrites outer variable!
  package = @hemPackage.compile()

hemPackage: ->
  package.create()
```

Global variables are needed from time to time, and to create those you need to set them as properties on `window`:

```
class window.Asset
  constructor: ->
```

By ensuring global variables are explicit, rather than implicit, CoffeeScript removes one of the major sources of bugs in JavaScript programs.

Semicolons

JavaScript does not enforce the use of semicolons in source code, so it's possible to omit them. However, behind the scenes, the JavaScript compiler still needs them, so the parser automatically inserts them whenever it encounters a parse error due to a missing semicolon. In other words, it'll try to evaluate a statement without semicolons and, if that fails, tries again using semicolons.

Unfortunately, this is a tremendously bad idea, and can actually change the behavior of your code. Take the following example, which seems like valid JavaScript, right?

```
function() {}
(window.options || {}).property
```

Wrong. Well, at least according to the parser; it raises a syntax error. In case of a leading parenthesis, the parser will not insert a semicolon. The code gets transformed onto one line:

```
function() {}(window.options || {}).property
```

Now you can see the issue, and why the parser is complaining. When you're writing JavaScript, you should always include semicolons after statements. Fortunately, CoffeeScript gets around all this hassle by not having semicolons in its syntax. Rather, the semicolons are inserted automatically (at the right places) when the CoffeeScript is compiled down to JavaScript.

Reserved Words

Certain keywords in JavaScript are reserved for future versions of JavaScript, such as `const`, `enum`, and `class`. Using these as variable names in your JavaScript programs can result in unpredictable results; some browsers will cope with them just fine, and others will choke. CoffeeScript neatly sidesteps this issue, by detecting if you're using a reserved keyword, and escaping it if necessary.

For example, let's say you were to use the reserved keyword `class` as a property on an object. Your CoffeeScript might look like this:

```
myObj = {
  delete: "I am a keyword!"
}
myObj.class = ->
```

The CoffeeScript parser notices you're using a reserved keyword, and quotes it for you:

```
var myObj;
myObj = {
  "delete": "I am a keyword!"
};
myObj["class"] = function() {};
```

Equality Comparisons

The weak equality comparison in JavaScript has some confusing behavior and is often the source of confusing bugs. The example below is taken from JavaScript Garden's equality section (*http://bonsaiden.github.com/JavaScript-Garden/#types.equality*), which delves into the issue in some depth:

```
""         ==    "0"        // false
0          ==    ""         // true
0          ==    "0"        // true
false      ==    "false"    // false
false      ==    "0"        // true
false      ==    undefined  // false
false      ==    null       // false
null       ==    undefined  // true
" \t\r\n"  ==    0          // true
```

The reason behind this behavior is that the weak equality coerces types automatically. I'm sure you'll agree this is all pretty ambiguous, and can lead to unexpected results and bugs.

The solution is to instead use the strict equality operator, which consists of three equal signs (===). It works exactly like the normal equality operator, but without any type coercion. It's recommended to always use the strict equality operator, and explicitly convert types if needs be.

CoffeeScript solves this by simply replacing all weak comparisons with strict ones (in other words, converting all == comparators into ===). You can't do a a weak equality comparison in CoffeeScript, and you should explicitly convert types before comparing them if necessary.

This doesn't mean you can ignore type coercion in CoffeeScript completely though, especially when it comes to checking the "truthfulness" of variables during flow control. Blank strings, `null`, `undefined`, and the number 0 are all coerced to `false`:

```
alert("Empty Array")  unless [].length
alert("Empty String") unless ""
alert("Number 0")     unless 0
```

If you want to explicitly check for null and undefined, then you can use CoffeeScript's existential operator:

```
alert("This is not called") unless ""?
```

The alert() in this example won't be called, as the empty string isn't equal to null.

Function Definition

Oddly enough, in JavaScript, functions can be defined after they're used. For example, the following runs absolutely fine, even though wem is defined after it's called:

```
wem();
function wem() {}
```

This is because of function scope. Functions get hoisted before the program's execution and as such are available everywhere in the scope they were defined in, even if called before the actual definition in the source. The trouble is, hoisting behavior differs between browser. For example:

```
if (true) {
  function declaration() {
    return "first";
  }
} else {
  function declaration() {
    return "second";
  }
}
declaration();
```

In some browsers (e.g., Firefox), declaration() will return "first", and in other browsers (e.g., Chrome), it'll return "second", even though it looks like the else statement is never run.

If you want to know more about declarative functions, then you should read Juriy Zaytsev's guide (*http://kangax.github.com/nfe/*), where he delves into the specifics. Suffice to say, they have fairly ambiguous behavior, and can lead to problems later down the road. All things considered, it's best to steer clear of them by using function expressions instead:

```
var wem = function(){};
wem();
```

CoffeeScript's approach to this is to remove declarative functions entirely, using function expressions instead.

Number Property Lookups

A flaw in JavaScript's parser means that the *dot notation* on numbers is interpreted as a floating point literal, rather than a property lookup. For example, the following Java-Script will cause a syntax error:

```
5.toString();
```

JavaScript's parser is looking for another number after the dot, and so raises an `Unexpected token` error when it encounters `toString()`. The solution to this is to either use parenthesis, or add an additional dot:

```
(5).toString();
5..toString();
```

Fortunately, CoffeeScript's parsers are clever enough to deal with this issue by using double dot notations automatically (as in the preceding example) whenever you access properties on numbers.

JavaScript Lint

JavaScript Lint (*http://www.javascriptlint.com/*) is a JavaScript code quality tool, and running your programs through it is a great way of improving code quality and best practices. The project was based on a similar tool called JSLint (*http://www.jslint .com*). Check out JSLint's site for a great list (*http://www.jslint.com/lint.html*) of issues that it checks for, including global variables, missing semicolons, and weak equality comparisons.

The good news is that CoffeeScript already "lints" all of its output, so CoffeeScript generated JavaScript is already JavaScript Lint compatible. In fact, the `coffee` tool has support for a `--lint` option:

```
coffee --lint index.coffee
  index.coffee: 0 error(s), 0 warning(s)
```

## CHAPTER 6

The Little Conclusion

By Jeremy Ashkenas[1]

You've reached the end of *The Little Book on CoffeeScript*, and now you know just about everything you'll need. CoffeeScript is a little language at heart, and if you know JavaScript and have a sense of the philosophy behind the changes that CoffeeScript makes to JavaScript, you should be able to get up and running very quickly indeed.

Philosophy

Unlike most programming languages, CoffeeScript was never designed from the ground up. It has always been an attempt to express core JavaScript concepts in as simple and minimal a syntax as we can find for them.

Let's take a simple function. To produce the square of x, we multiply x by itself. In JavaScript:

```
var square = function(x) {
  return x * x;
};
```

To derive the CoffeeScript for this, let's think through the steps it would take to reduce this function to its essential features.

- We can understand the code perfectly well without the semicolons, so let's drop those.

- Instead of using { and } to delimit the body of the function, let's use the indentation that's already present on the page.

- It's clear that we're defining a new function, so let's drop the redundant **var** in front of the assignment.

---

1. This last chapter was kindly contributed by Jeremy Ashkenas, the author of CoffeeScript.

- Every construct in CoffeeScript should be an expression with a value, so the natural value of a function body is the last line of code it executes ... allowing us to omit the `return`.
- Finally, we replace `function( input ){ output }` with a function literal that visually represents the idea that the input of a function "points to" the output: `(input) -> output`.

Voilá, the CoffeeScript version:

```
square = (x) -> x * x
```

Every language feature in CoffeeScript has been designed using this kind of process: attempt to take the beautiful dynamic semantics of JavaScript—object literals, function expressions, prototypal inheritance—and express them in a clean, readable, minimal way.

It's Just JavaScript

CoffeeScript tries to be a deeply pragmatic language. To be honest, it's probably too pragmatic for its own good. The golden rule of CoffeeScript is: "It's just JavaScript."

We want to embrace the limitations of compiling to JavaScript by only implementing things that can be expressed in simple JS, and leaving fancier compilations to other languages (*https://github.com/jashkenas/coffee-script/wiki/List-of-languages-that-com pile-to-JS*). When you run a script, there is no CoffeeScript interpreter running within the browser, no core library you have to include on the page, and ideally (although we bend this rule in a few places) no special helper functions generated alongside your code.

The downside of this approach is that more invasive improvements to JavaScript are impossible. For example, it would be nice if `list[-1]` in CoffeeScript could return the last item in the list. At first glance, it seems simple enough to implement, and would be useful. Unfortunately, any expression may be used to index into an array, so with negative array indices you would have to add a special check to every `list[x]` operation to ask if `x` is a positive number or a negative one. This would take CoffeeScript away from JavaScript semantics, and more importantly, JavaScript levels of performance—the array accesses in your inner loops would slow down considerably. For this reason, CoffeeScript doesn't add negative array indices to the language.

The upside of this approach is that CoffeeScript is inherently compatible with every JavaScript runtime. Because we can compile to efficient, lowest-common-denominator code, CoffeeScript runs as well as JavaScript in every browser, in Node.js, in Rhino, in Photoshop and Illustrator—in short, everywhere JavaScript can run. If you want to use CoffeeScript for a project, for a component, or even just for a single file, you don't have to sacrifice performance or compatibility with other JavaScript libraries.

Build Your Own JavaScript

There's a hidden motive running as a subtext beneath CoffeeScript. I hope that this book doesn't merely serve as an introduction, but spurs you to experiment with compile-to-JavaScript languages of your very own.

To that end, the CoffeeScript compiler has been fully annotated with commentary (*http://coffeescript.org/documentation/docs/grammar.html*) to make it easier to get started prototyping changes and improvements. The entire thing is only around 2,500 lines of code, and there have been a number (*https://github.com/satyr/coco*) of interesting (*http://weepy.github.com/kaffeine/*) forks (*http://disnetdev.com/contracts.coffee/*) already that push JavaScript in different directions.

If you've ever felt confined by JavaScript, there's no need to wait around for browser implementors or the slow march of the standards process. By using a compile-to-JS language, you can give yourself the JavaScript of your dreams today. I'm looking forward to seeing more little languages out there in the wild soon.

About the Author

Alex MacCaw is a Ruby/JavaScript developer and entrepreneur. He has written a JavaScript framework, Spine, and developed major applications including Taskforce and Socialmod, as well as a host of open source work. He has spoken at Ruby/Rails conferences in New York City, San Francisco, and Berlin. In addition to programming, he is currently traveling around the world with a Nikon D90 and surfboard.

Get even more for your money.

Join the O'Reilly Community, and register the O'Reilly books you own. It's free, and you'll get:

- $4.99 ebook upgrade offer
- 40% upgrade offer on O'Reilly print books
- Membership discounts on books and events
- Free lifetime updates to ebooks and videos
- Multiple ebook formats, DRM FREE
- Participation in the O'Reilly community
- Newsletters
- Account management
- 100% Satisfaction Guarantee

Signing up is easy:

1. **Go to: oreilly.com/go/register**
2. **Create an O'Reilly login.**
3. **Provide your address.**
4. **Register your books.**

Note: English-language books only

To order books online:
oreilly.com/store

For questions about products or an order:
orders@oreilly.com

To sign up to get topic-specific email announcements and/or news about upcoming books, conferences, special offers, and new technologies:
elists@oreilly.com

For technical questions about book content:
booktech@oreilly.com

To submit new book proposals to our editors:
proposals@oreilly.com

O'Reilly books are available in multiple DRM-free ebook formats. For more information:
oreilly.com/ebooks

O'REILLY®

Spreading the knowledge of innovators | oreilly.com

The information you need, when and where you need it.

With Safari Books Online, you can:

Access the contents of thousands of technology and business books

- Quickly search over 7000 books and certification guides
- Download whole books or chapters in PDF format, at no extra cost, to print or read on the go
- Copy and paste code
- Save up to 35% on O'Reilly print books
- **New!** Access mobile-friendly books directly from cell phones and mobile devices

Stay up-to-date on emerging topics before the books are published

- Get on-demand access to evolving manuscripts.
- Interact directly with authors of upcoming books

Explore thousands of hours of video on technology and design topics

- Learn from expert video tutorials
- Watch and replay recorded conference sessions

O'REILLY®

CPSIA information can be obtained at www.ICGtesting.com
Printed in the USA
BVOW081219190212

283280BV00002B/6/P

9 781449 321055